MW00975541

MAR 17 2004

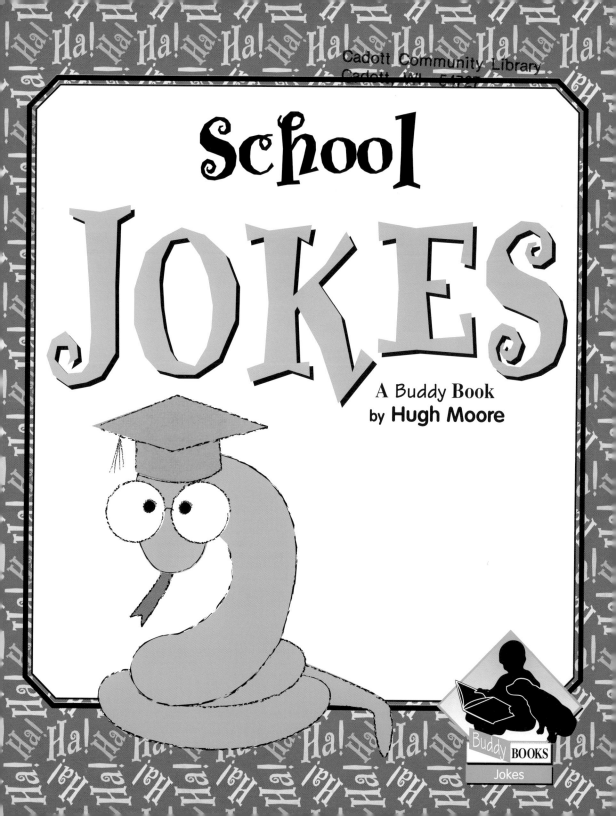

# School

# JOKES

A Buddy Book
by Hugh Moore

Buddy BOOKS

Jokes

VISIT US AT

www.abdopub.com

Published by ABDO Publishing Company, 4940 Viking Drive, Suite 622, Edina, Minnesota 55435.

Printed in the United States.

Edited by: Sarah Tieck
Contributing Editors: Matt Ray, Michael P. Goecke
Graphic Design: Deborah Coldiron
Illustrations by: Deborah Coldiron and Maria Hosley

## Library of Congress Cataloging-in-Publication Data

Moore, Hugh, 1970-
  School jokes/Hugh Moore.
     p. cm. — (Jokes)
  Includes index.
  ISBN 1-59197-626-X
     1. Schools—Juvenile humor. 2. Education—Juvenile humor. [1. Schools—Humor.
  2. Education—Humor. 3. Jokes.] I. Title. II. Series.

PN6231.S3M66 2004
818'.602—dc22

                                                    2003063616

# Why was 6 afraid of 7?

Because 7 ate 9!

What animal gets in trouble when it takes a test?

The cheetah!

Why did the prince bring his father to school?

The teacher said to bring a ruler!

Why don't you see giraffes in elementary school?

Because they're all in HIGH school!

Why are kindergarten teachers so great?

Because they know how to make little things count.

What is worse than finding a worm in your apple?

Finding half a worm in your apple!

Why was there thunder and lightning in the science lab?

The scientists were brainstorming!

What is the difference between a teacher and a train?

A teacher says, "Spit out your gum." A train says, "Chew chew!"

Why did the report card sting the girl?

It was full of Bs!

Why was the math teacher crying?

She had too many problems!

What has wings and solves
number problems?

A moth-ematician!

# What is a snake's favorite subject?

Hiss-tory!

Why were the early days of history called the dark ages?

Because there were so many knights!

At what school do you have to drop out so you can graduate?

Parachute school!

Why did the children wear their swimsuits to school?

They rode in a car pool!

What is the difference between a teacher and a train's engineer?

One trains minds, the other minds trains!

**Student:** Hello? I'm calling because my son has a bad cold and won't be able to come to school today.
**School secretary:** Who is this?
**Student:** This is my father speaking!

Why does history keep repeating itself?

Because we weren't listening the first time!

**Teacher:** Class, we will have only half a day of school this morning.
**Class:** Yay!
**Teacher:** We'll have the other half this afternoon!

What did the turtle wear to keep warm on his walk to school?

A turtleneck!

Why did the teacher marry the janitor?

Because he swept her off her feet!

Student: Lunch lady, this soup tastes funny.
Lunch Lady: Then why aren't you laughing?

What is the easiest way to raise your grades?

Hold them up in the air!

Mom: What did you learn in school today?
Son: How to write.
Mom: What did you write?
Son: I don't know, we're learning to read tomorrow!

Teacher: Why is the Mississippi such an unusual river?
Student: Because it has four eyes and still can't see!

Why did the math teacher take a ruler to bed?

To see how long she slept!

Why did the teacher yell at Humpty Dumpty?

He cracked up during class!

What two letters can keep you from doing your homework?

TV!

# What did Caesar say to Cleopatra?

Toga-ther we can rule the world!

What happened to the frog that
was parked in front of the school?

His car got toad away!

Why did the teacher wear sunglasses?

Because his class was so bright!

Why was the chicken thrown out of school?

It used fowl language!

Teacher: Where is your homework?
Student: I lost it fighting a kid who said you weren't the best teacher in the school!

What must you pay to go to school?

Attention!

How is a teacher like an eye doctor?

They both examine pupils!

How do students get to school in the fall?

By autumn-obile!

What kind of food does a math teacher bring in her lunch box?

A square meal!

18

How do bees get to school?

What did the spider do on the computer?

Made a web site!

What is a teacher's favorite candy?

Chalk-olate!

What exam do young witches have to pass?

A spell-ing test!

Why did the boy eat his homework?

Because his teacher said it was a piece of cake!

Teacher: I hope I didn't see you looking at Johnny's test.
Student: I hope you didn't see me either!

Why are fish so smart?

Because they live in schools.

Why is the library the tallest room in the school?

It has the most stories!

What is an astronaut's favorite part of a computer?

The space bar!

How do you make a band stand?

Take away their chairs!

# What is the best thing to eat when you are behind on your homework?

# Web Sites